The Resolving Bereave

First published 2010 by
Veritas Publications
7–8 Lower Abbey Street
Dublin 1
Ireland
publications@veritas.ie
www.veritas.ie

ISBN 978 1 84730 254 0

Copyright © Fiona McAuslan and Peter Nicholson, 2010

10 9 8 7 6 5 4 3 2 1

The material in this publication is protected by copyright law. Except as may be permitted by law, no part of the material may be reproduced (including by storage in a retrieval system) or transmitted in any form or by any means, adapted, rented or lent without the written permission of the copyright owners. Applications for permissions should be addressed to the publisher.

A catalogue record for this book is available from the British Library.

Designed by Kelly Sheridan
Printed in the Republic of Ireland by Walsh Colour Print, Kerry

Veritas books are printed on paper made from the wood pulp of managed forests. For every tree felled, at least one tree is planted, thereby renewing natural resources.

About the Authors

Fiona McAuslan holds a Masters in Mediation and Conflict Resolution Studies from University College Dublin. She is an experienced mediator and conflict coach with many years' experience working with family, workplace and school conflicts. She works in the Irish Family Mediation Service and Clanwilliam Institute and is an accredited Practitioner Mediator with the Mediators Institute of Ireland. Fiona has published the S.A.L.T. Programme: A Conflict Resolution Education Programme for Primary Schools. She lives in North County Dublin with her husband, Michael, and two children, Sarah and Ben.

Peter Nicholson is a communications specialist and has built a very successful Marketing and Visual Communications Business over the last fifteen years. Peter has worked on many self-help publications and met Fiona whilst working on the S.A.L.T. Programme, and they have continued to work together on many other projects. He is married to Karen, and they have two fantastic friends who happen to be their children, Patrick and Ailish.

About the Illustrator

Kelly Sheridan studied Classical and Computer Animation in Ballyfermot College of Further Education for three years before attending the Irish Academy of Computer Training (IACT) to study Graphic Design and Desktop Publishing. Kelly now has a very successful career as a graphic designer and illustrator. She lives in South Dublin with her partner and best friend, Mark.

The Resolving Bereavement Book

Read Me First!

This is not just another story book, it's a Tool Book. So what's a Tool Book then? It's a book that explains an issue, shows how children can be affected by it and how they can resolve the problem. It also offers a number of tips and techniques that can be used again and again to improve a child's ability to deal with bereavement and grief on a day-to-day basis.

Section 1
What are Bereavement and Grief?
This is a simple explanation of what bereavement and grief are.

Section 2
The Story
The story helps the reader talk about bereavement in their world and helps open the door to discussing and resolving their grief issues.

Section 3
Tool Box
The Tool Box has many tips and techniques that can be used in everyday life on an ongoing basis. The more they are practised, the better the result!

The Resolving BEREAVEMENT Grief with your Child Book

What are Bereavement and Grief?

Grief is a natural feeling. We cannot ignore it or pretend that we don't feel it.

More info VISIT www.resolvingbooks.com/typesofgrief

The Resolving Bereavement Book

Bereavement is the word we use when we lose someone we love and **grief** is a deep sadness we feel when someone we love dies or goes away.

We can also feel grief when our family life changes - when parents separate or the family moves to a new place.

We can start feeling better when we talk about it.

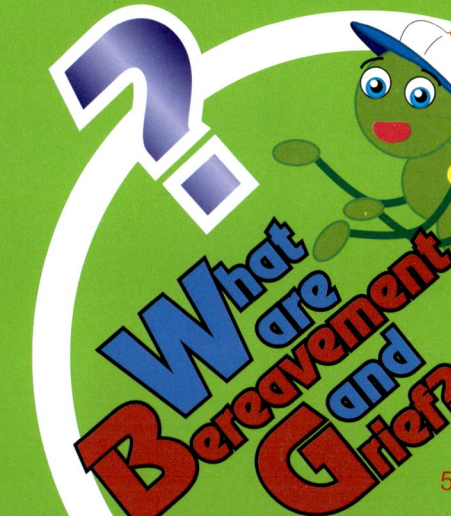

What are Bereavement and Grief?

The Resolving BEREAVEMENT Grief with your Child Book

How Grief Can Make You Feel

Sad

Ill

Frightened

Anxious

Isolated

Unconfident

The Resolving Bereavement Book

Lonely

Angry

Nervous

Guilty

Clingy

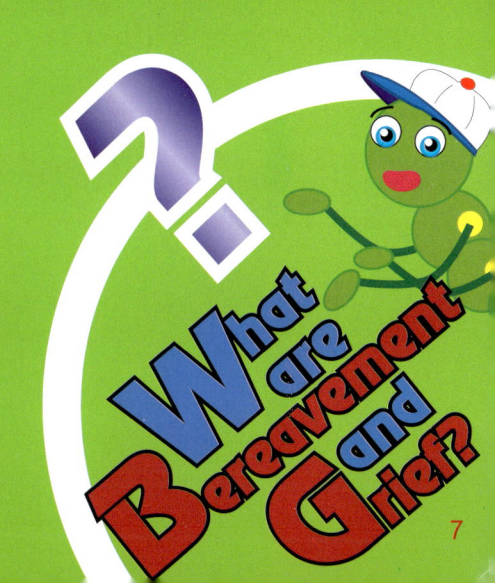

What are Bereavement and Grief?

Feelings

Everyone has feelings. They are part of our everyday life and are neither good nor bad. Feelings can be confusing and sometimes it can be hard to know how we actually feel. How we express our feelings is important.

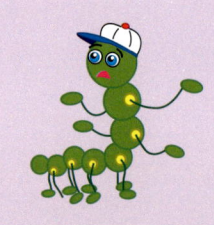

The Resolving Bereavement Book

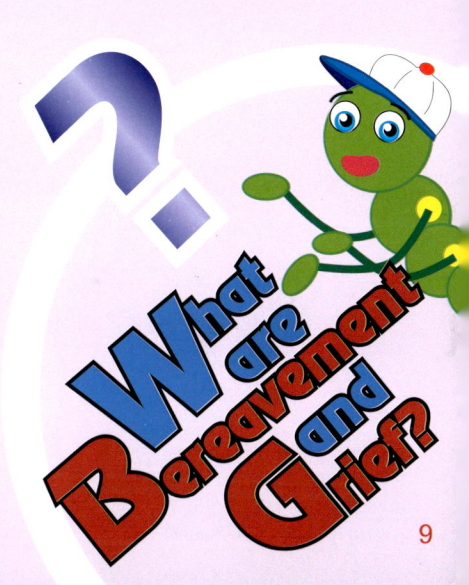

What are Bereavement and Grief?

The Resolving BEREAVEMENT Grief with your Child Book

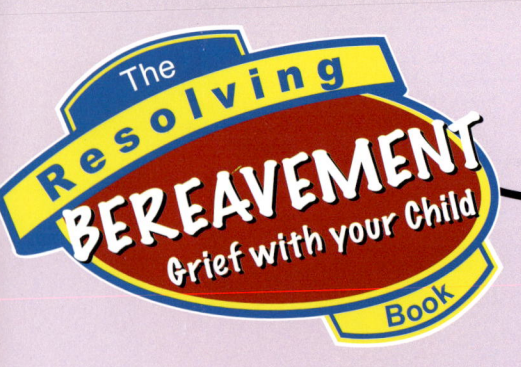

When someone we love dies we feel very sad for a long time. Sometimes we can feel very alone and think we will never be happy again.

The Resolving Bereavement Book

However, death is part of life and with time we will start feeling better. We can remember the person through our memories.

What are Bereavement and Grief?

This is Lisa

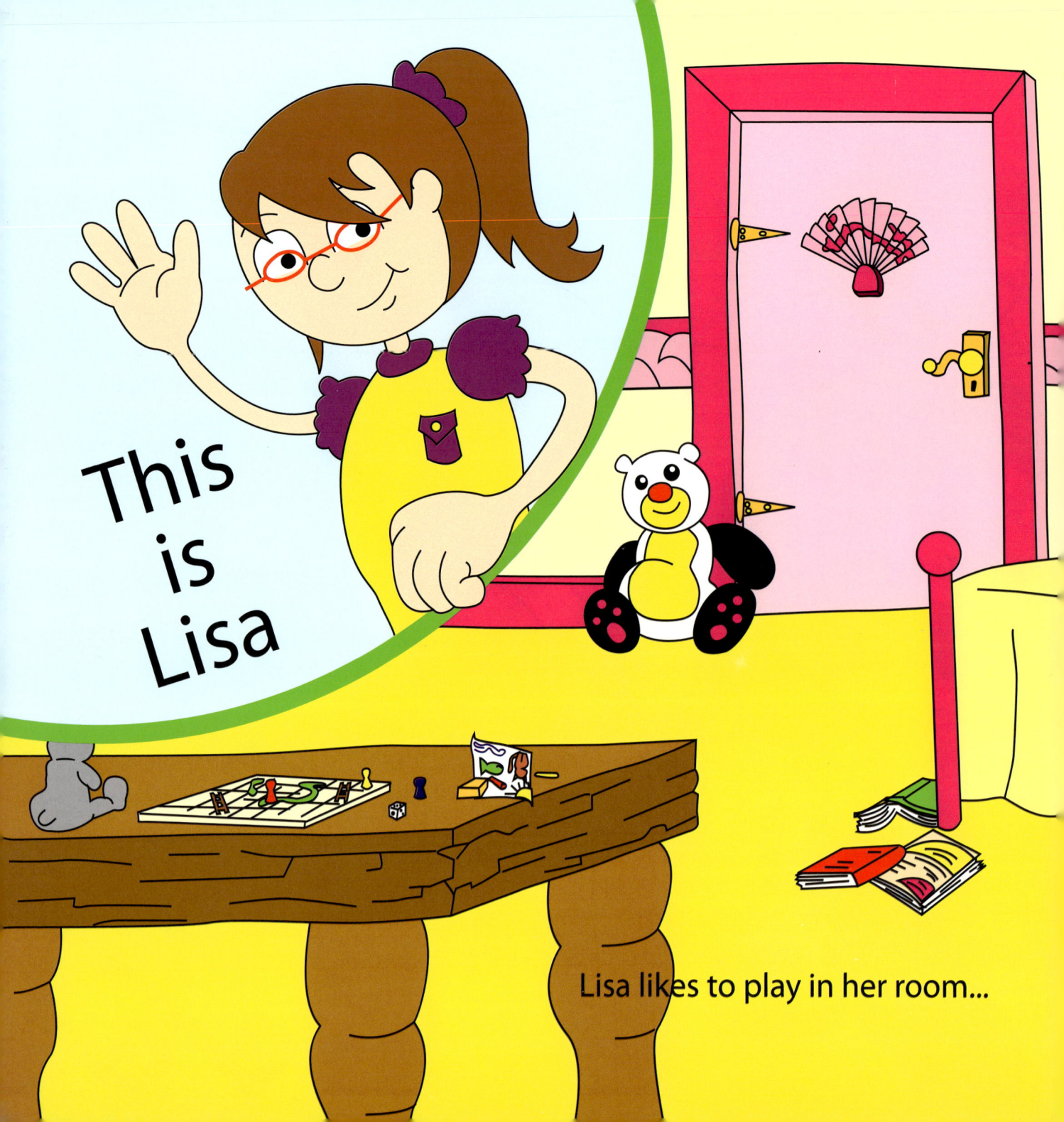

Lisa likes to play in her room...

but sometimes she feels sad.

Lisa felt too sad
to play with her friends...

or watch TV.

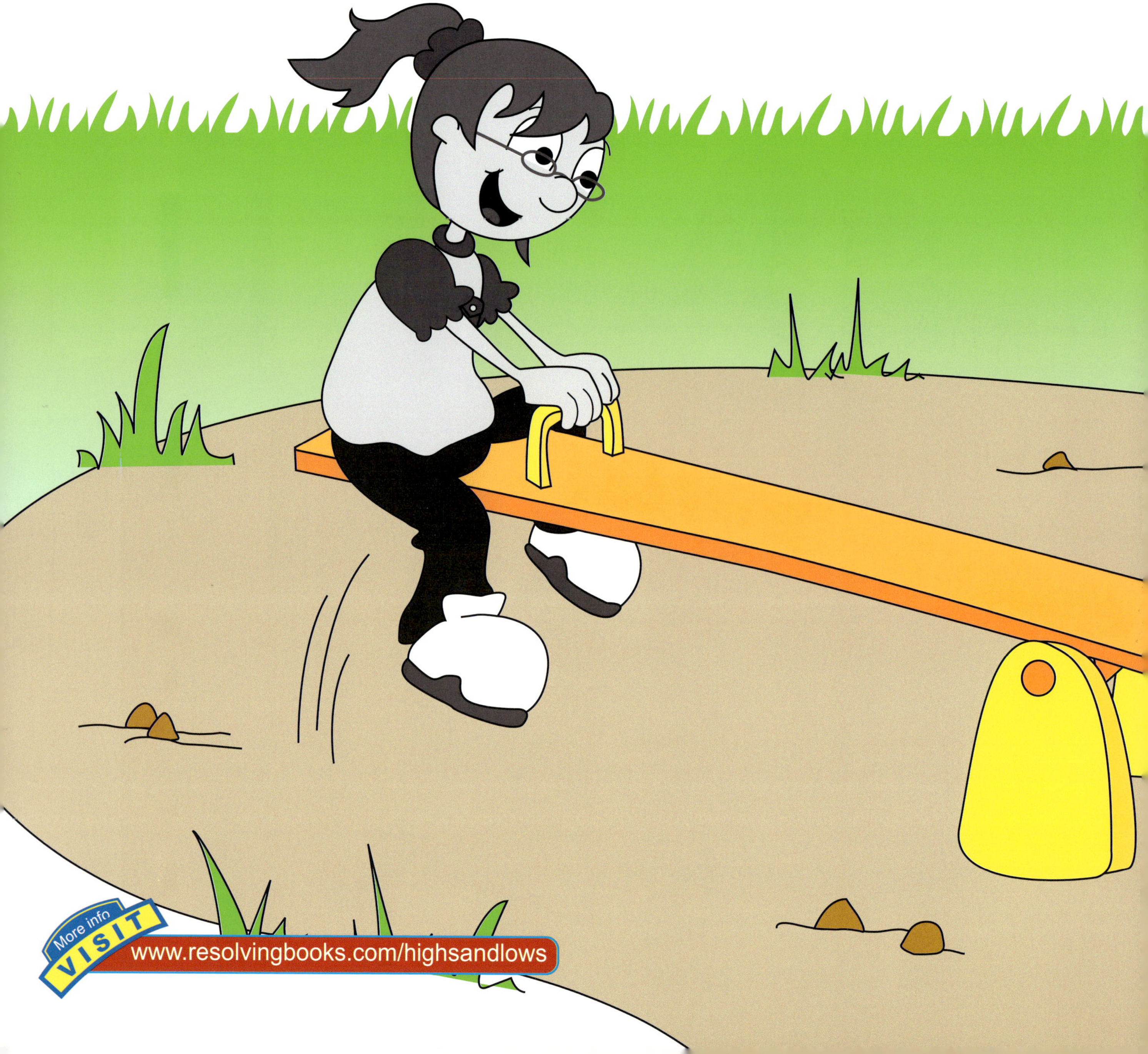

Sometimes she felt happy and wanted to play.

Then she would remember...

that her Mum had died.

Lisa's life had changed.

She hurt inside and didn't know what to do.

Lisa felt lonely. She worried a lot.

She thought she might have done something wrong. She longed for her Mum to be with her.

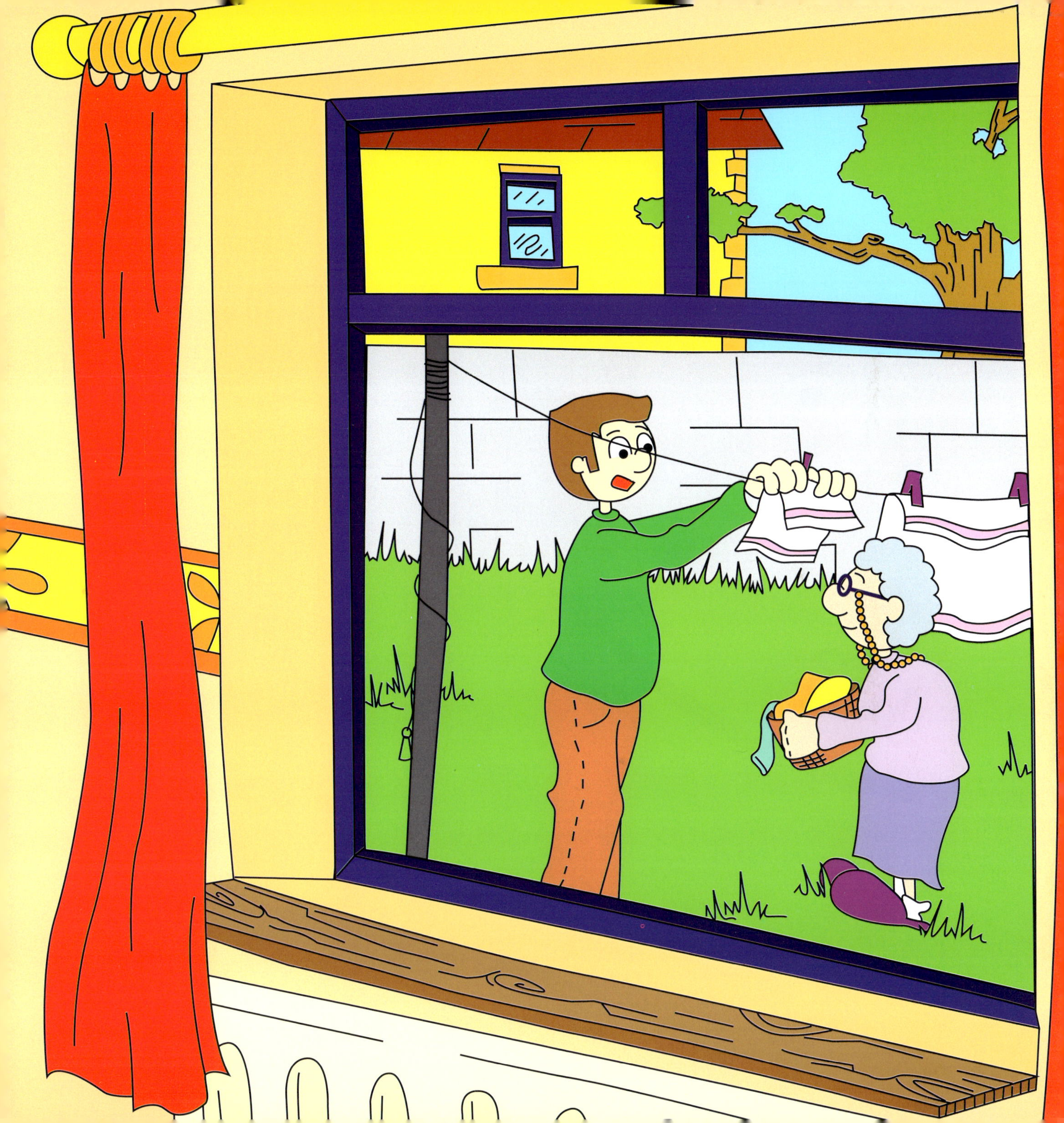

This is Joe

Joe loves playing basketball and drawing pictures.

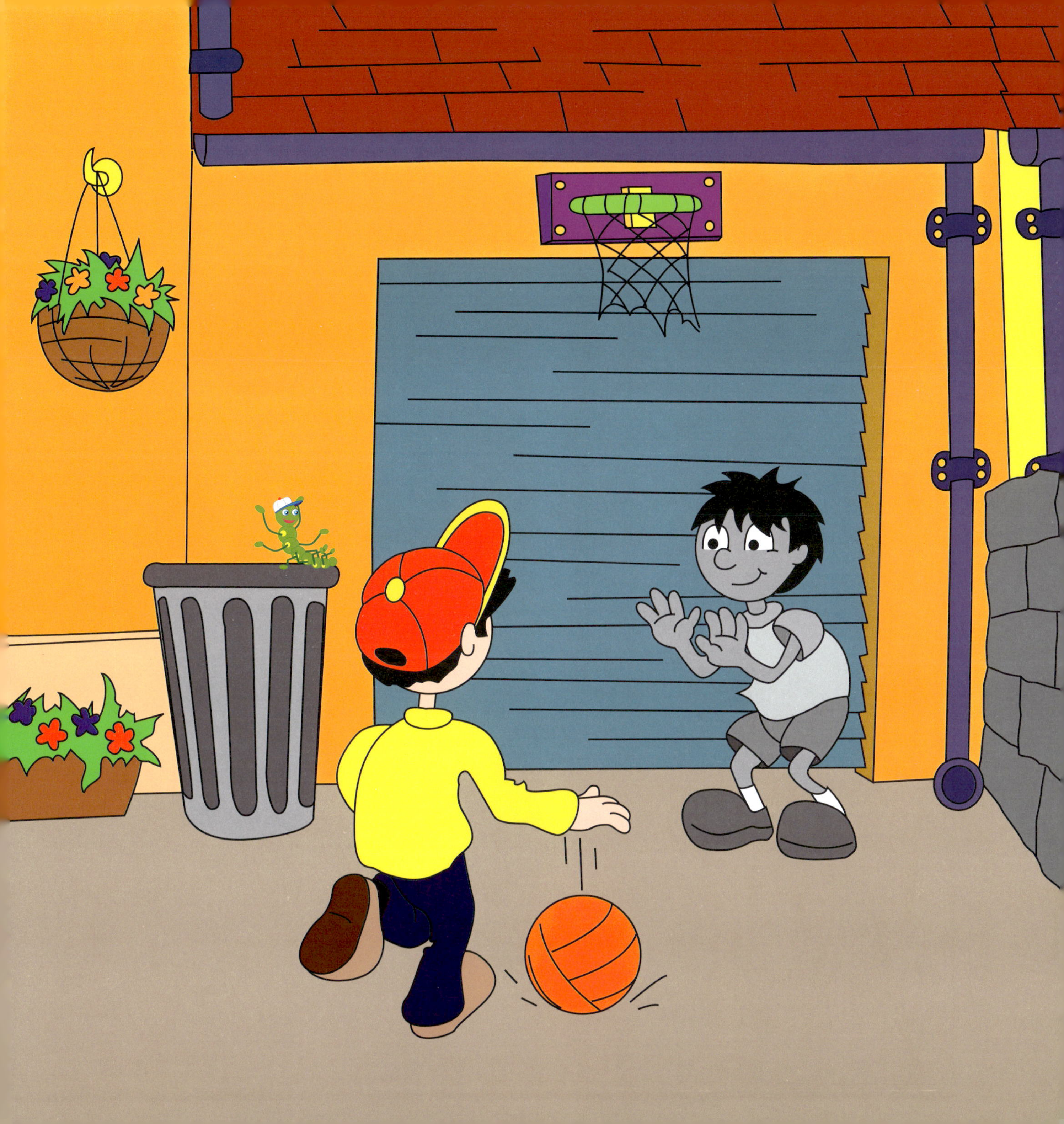

He has lots of friends
and enjoyed being with them...

but now he finds it hard to get on with them.

Sometimes Joe got so angry...

"I did score!!"

he felt he would explode.

Sometimes he hated his life.

I'M GOING HOME!

He felt so alone and angry.

Poor Joe.
He did not understand what was wrong.

His Dad had gone. He had died some time ago. His Mum said he was not coming back. Joe was so angry.

www.resolvingbooks.com/discussingloss

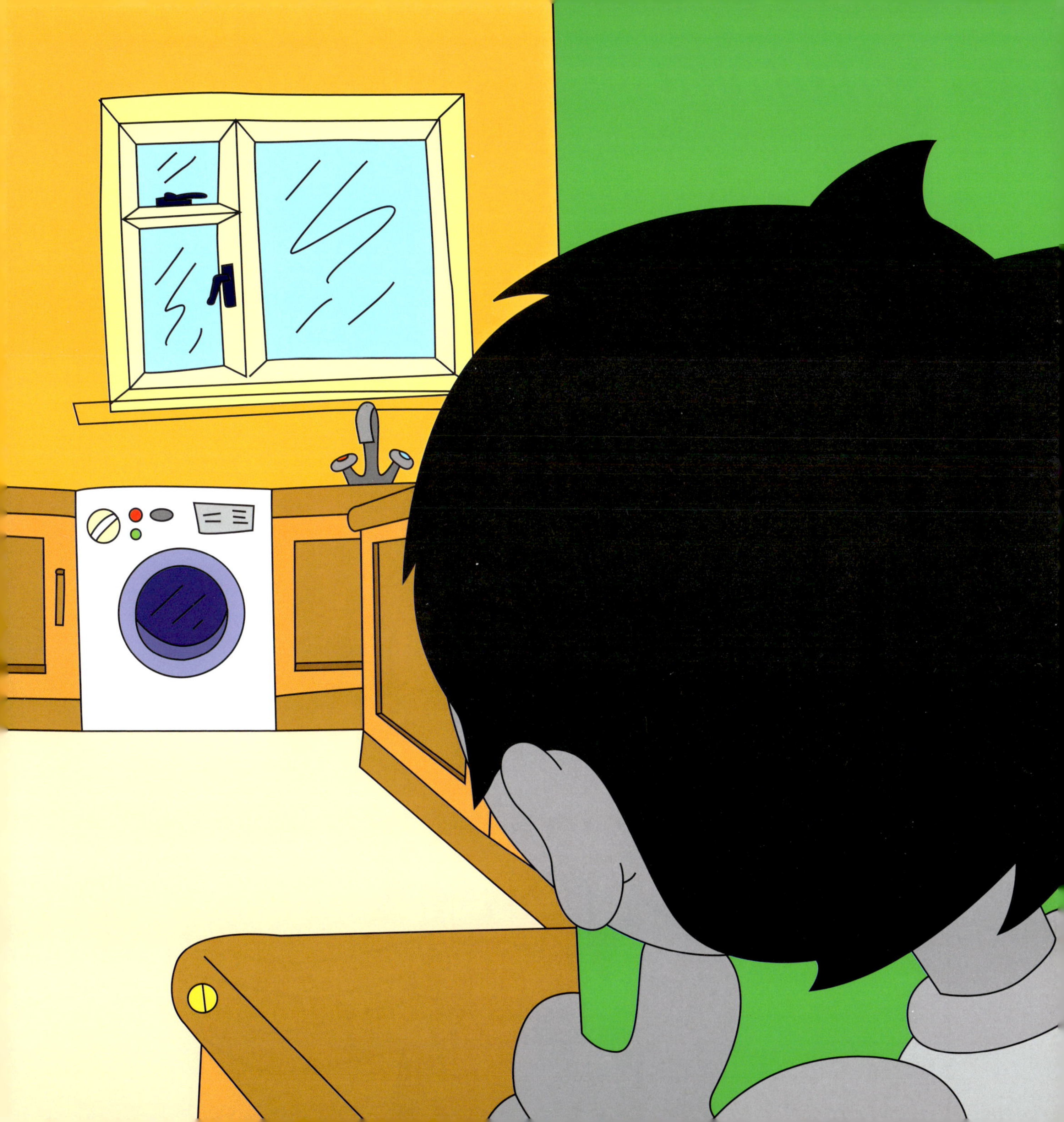

Lisa and Joe both went to the same school.

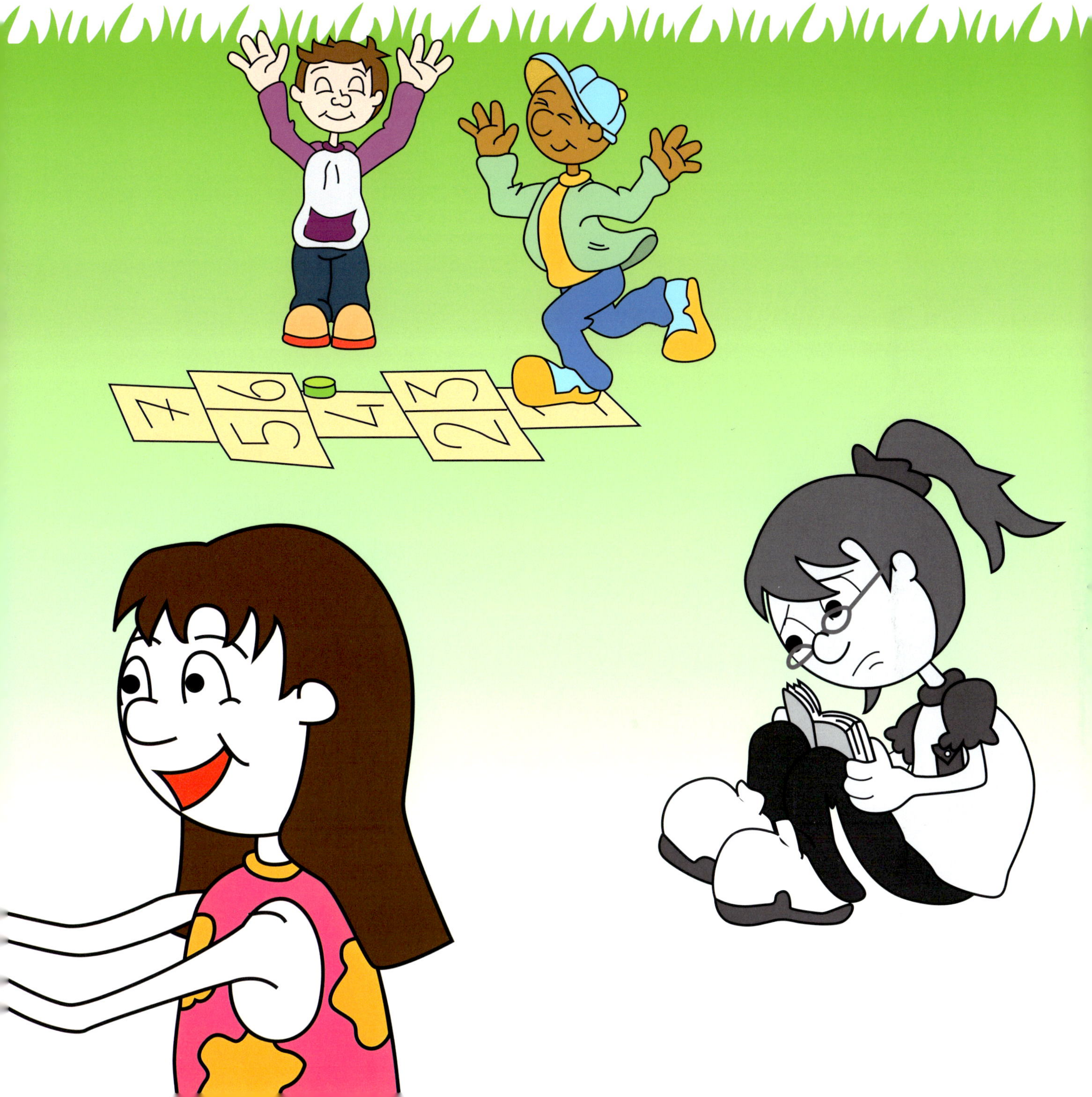

Each day they were busy.

Lisa liked writing stories. Joe thought science was cool.

www.resolvingbooks.com/whenwelosesomeone

But some days were hard.

Some days Lisa just wanted to cry and cry.
She felt so upset. There was nothing anyone could do.

Joe wanted to scream and shout.
He felt so angry that his Dad had left him.

AARGH!!!

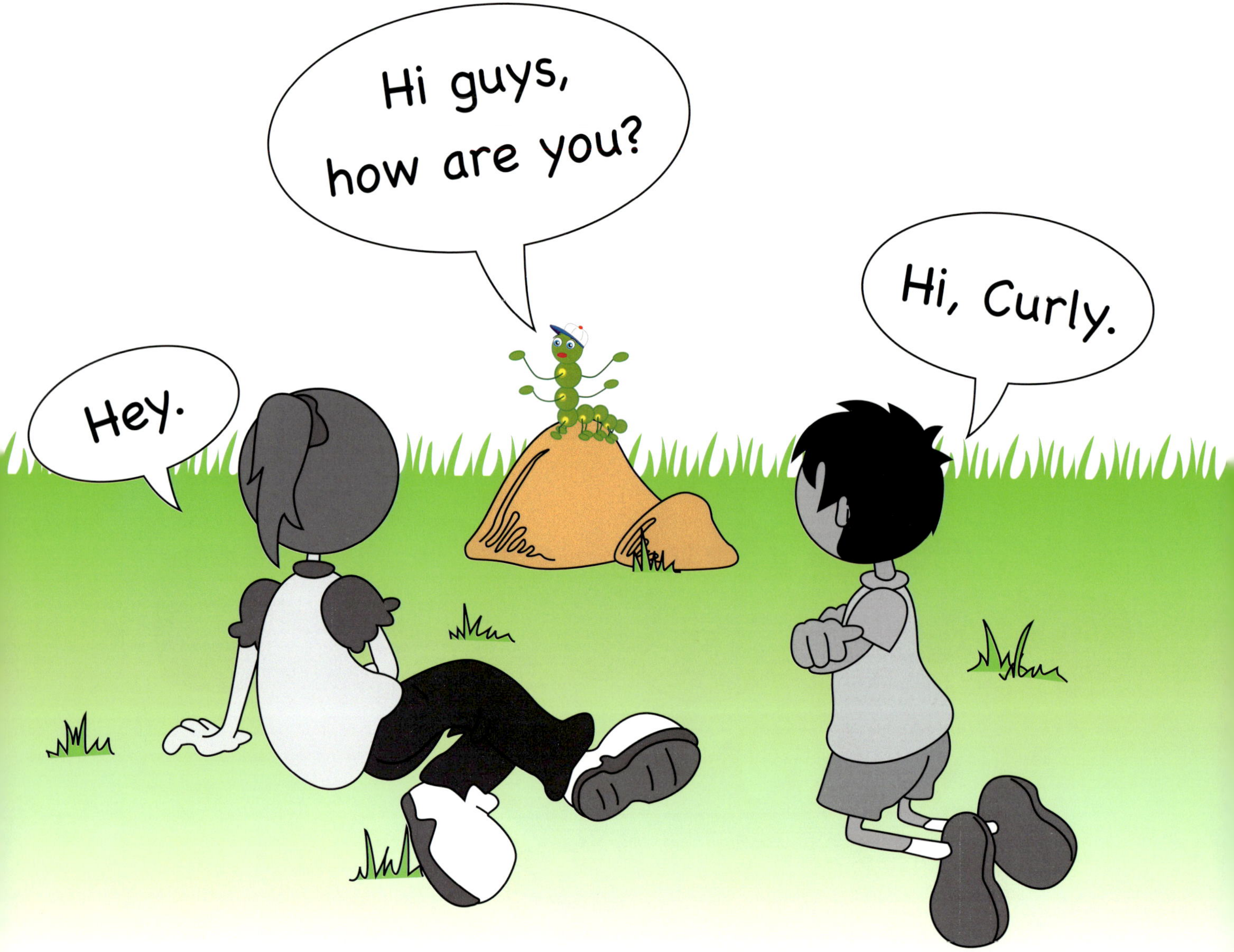
Hey.
Hi guys, how are you?
Hi, Curly.

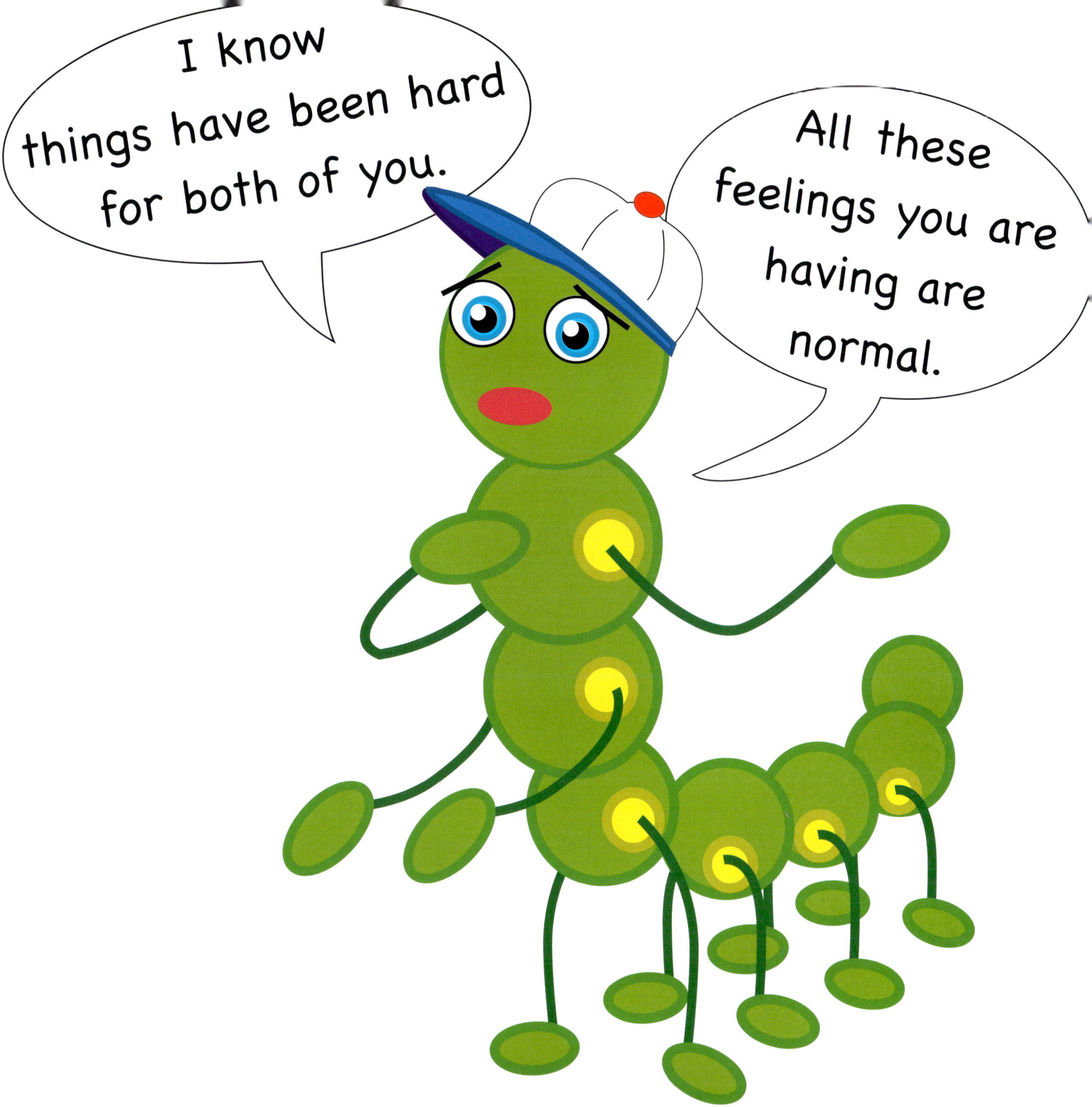
I know things have been hard for both of you.
All these feelings you are having are normal.

When we lose someone we love, we miss them very much. It can really hurt. It is called 'grieving'.
Is that why I feel so upset?

And why I miss my Dad so much?

We feel lots of different feelings when we lose someone and it's helpful to talk about them.
More info
VISIT
www.resolvingbooks.com/howpeoplefeelontheinside

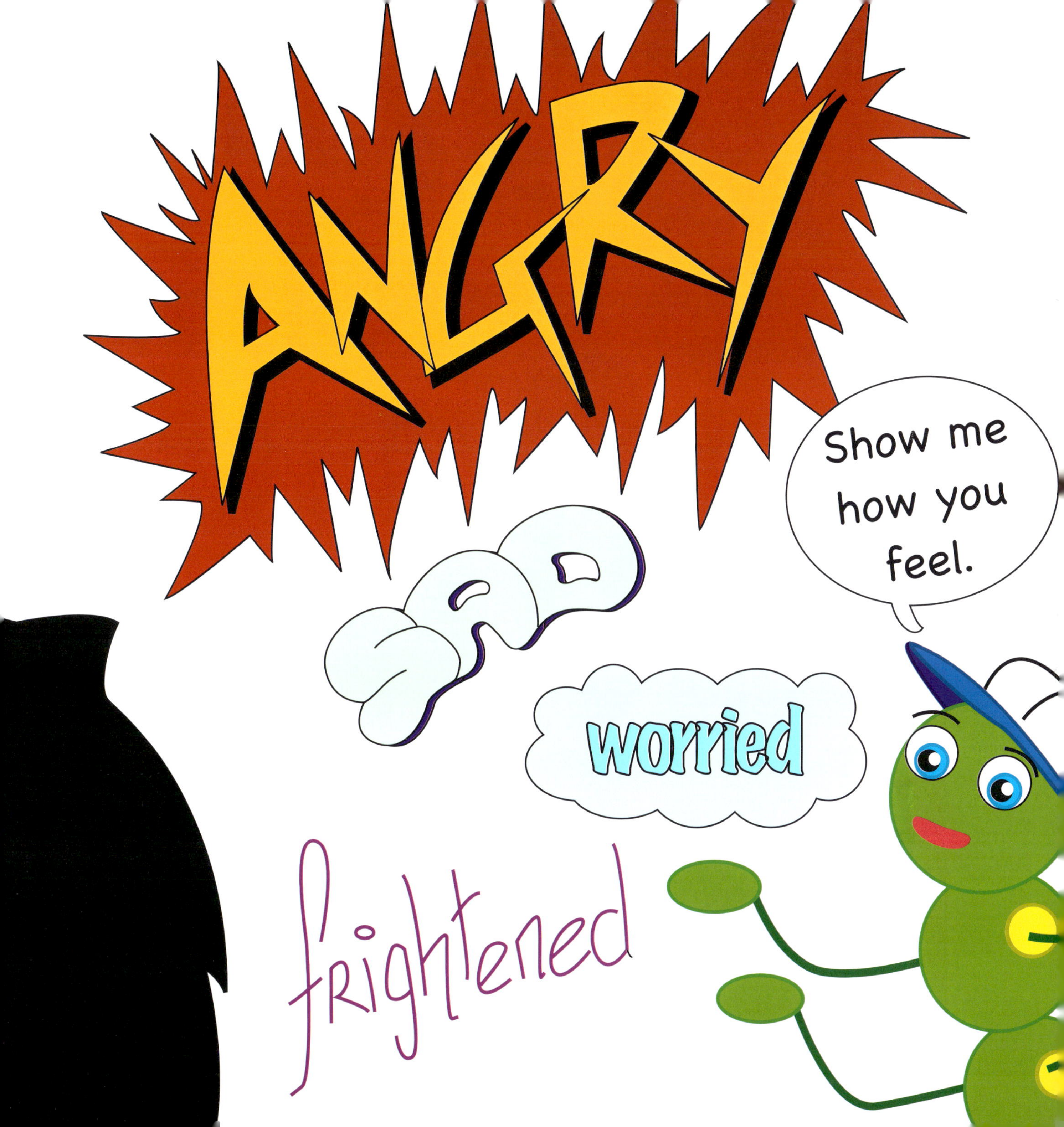
ANGRY
SAD
worried
frightened
Show me how you feel.

I feel sad inside.

I don't know what I'm supp[osed]

I worry.

I want to talk about my mum.

What's going to happen to me?

osed to do.

I say I'm fine but I'm not.

Sometimes I forget what Dad looked like.

Wow! I didn't know I had these feelings in me.
Neither did I. Now what do we do?

"Well, now you keep talking and find ways to help yourselves."

Why don't you make memory books?
What's a memory book?
It's a special book to put memories in.
I'd like to do that.

me and Mum at seaside

Our house

Dad

My Hero.
My dad is
My hero. He
is great. He
likes foot
and he w
when he

My M
cake a
do I. S
baked c
Sundays
me. We used eggs
and flour and milk.

Me and
Mum went
to the beach.
She taught
me how to
swim in the
sea. Th

FATHER + SON Relay Race

CINEMA TICKET
1 ADULT
1 CH

This
on

As they made their books they began to chat about their memories.

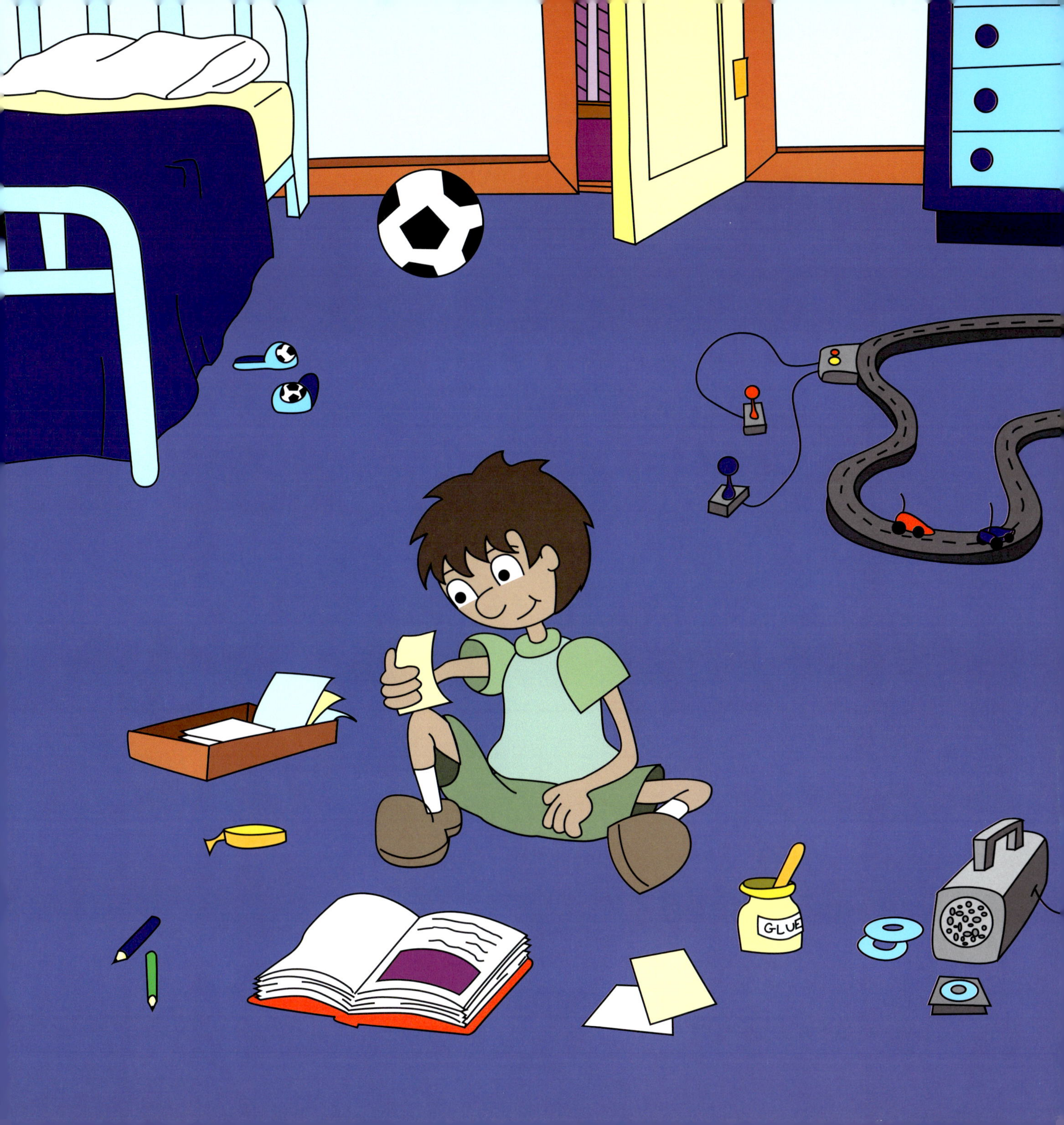
GLUE

My Dad always sang in the shower! Ha ha!
My Mum was funny when she danced... and she loved reading me stories.
We played ball every Saturday.

"It's funny, sometimes I forget what she looks like."

"Yes, me too..."

"Talking helps us begin to feel better."

Over the next few months, Lisa and Joe talked and talked...

They shared many happy and sad stories about how they felt.

"Dad, I don't want to make you sad but I really miss Mum."

"I miss her too, Lisa."

"Here's a picture of you and Mum from the day you were born."

They still had down days.

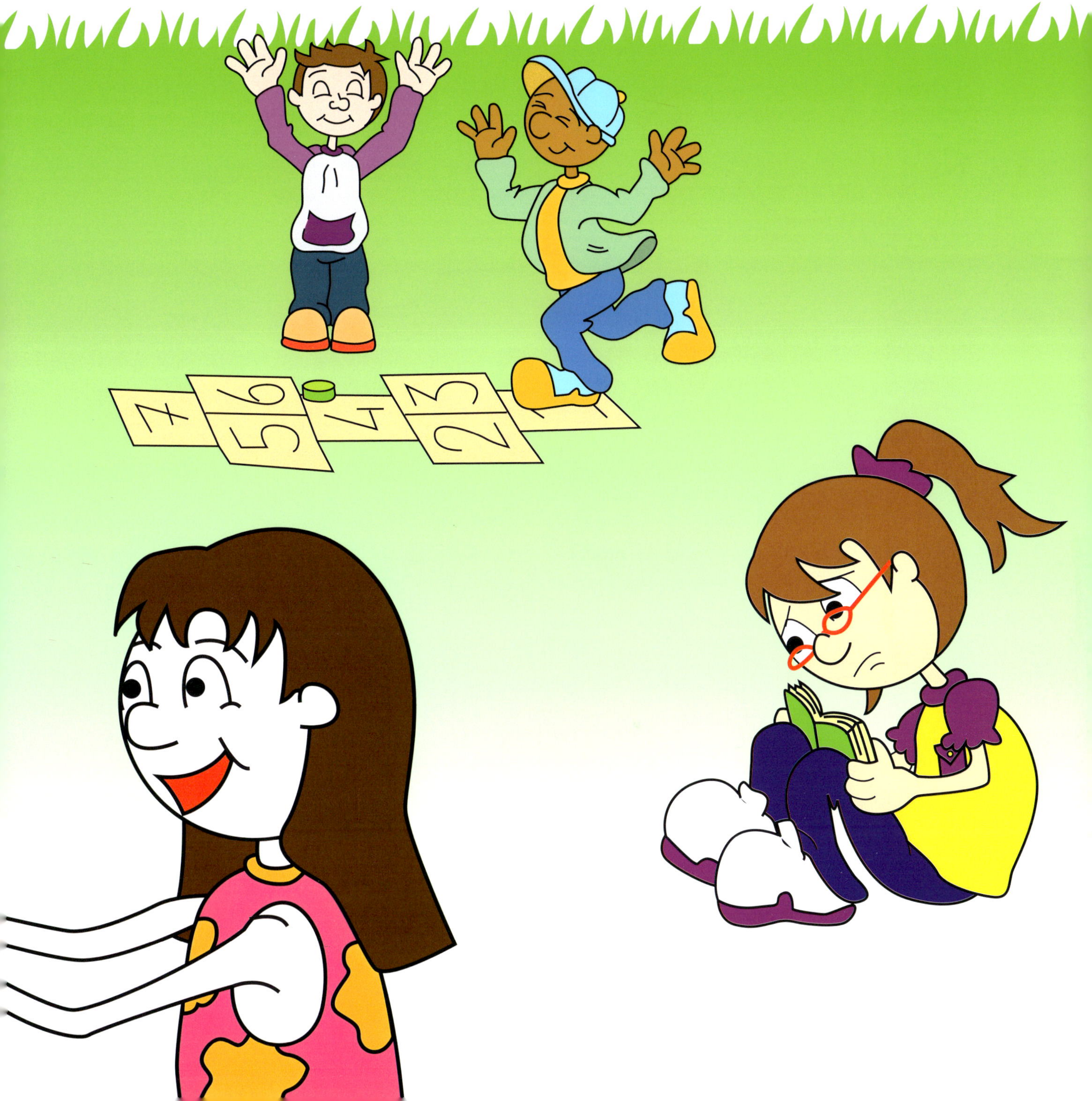

But they knew they would be alright...

and they had friends and family who cared.

www.resolvingbooks.com/support

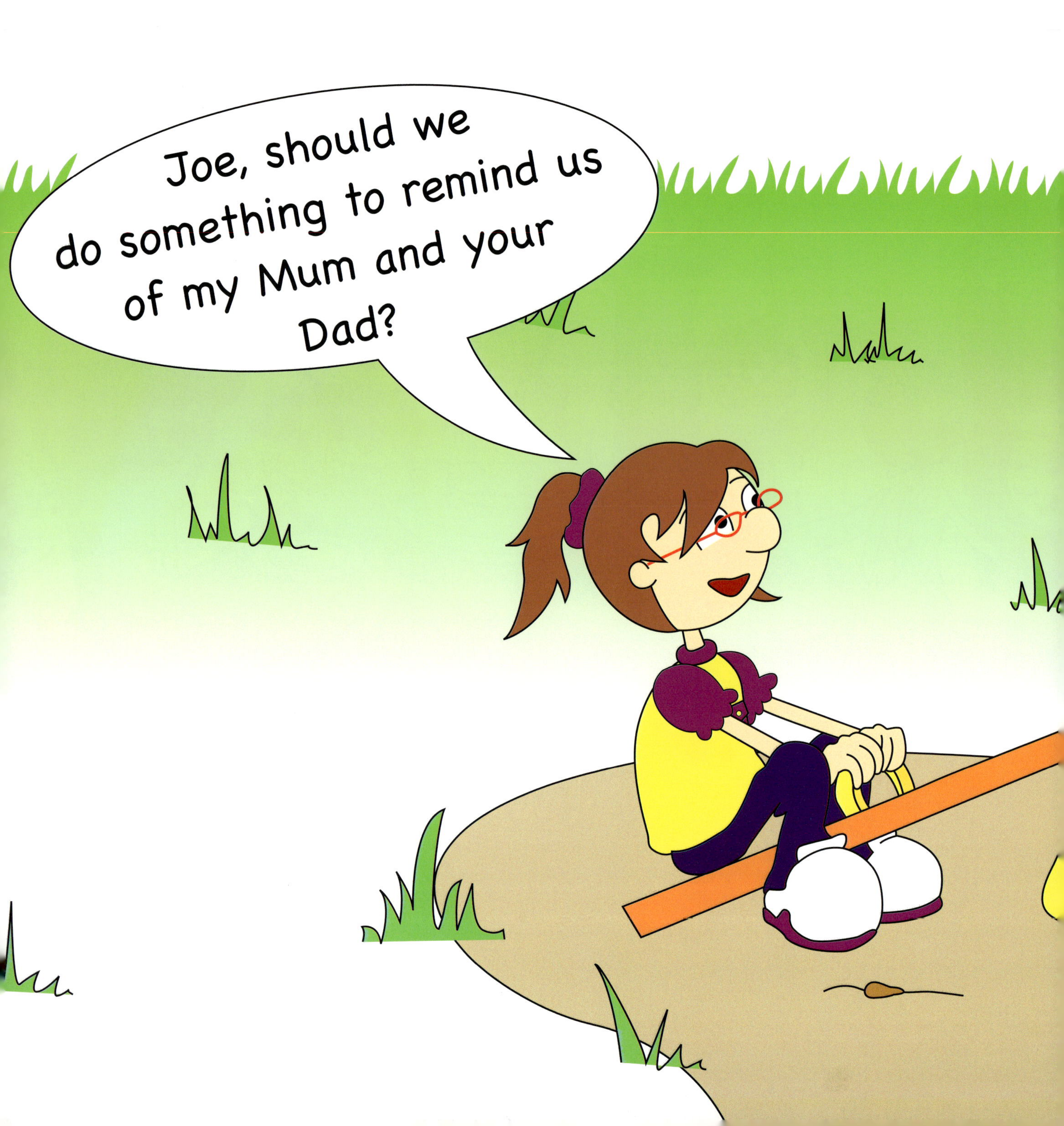
Joe, should we do something to remind us of my Mum and your Dad?

What do you mean?
What about somewhere you can go and remember them?

Joe helped Lisa plant a tree in her back garden.

"Mum liked apple trees."

She would think of all the happy times she had with her Mum as she watched it grow.

www.resolvingbooks.com/whydontyoutrythese

Then Lisa helped Joe make a corner of his room special with photos and pictures that reminded him of his Dad.

He liked to have somewhere quiet to go sometimes.

Hi, Curly!
How are you two?
We are ok. I still miss my Mum but I am not worrying as much.

Are you still feeling angry, Joe?
Not the way I used to. I feel better.

Sometimes you may feel down, but those times will get easier.

You will be ok.

The people we love will always be part of us.

The Resolving BEREAVEMENT Grief with your Child Book

Curly

Listens

More info VISIT www.resolvingbooks.com/thecaterpillar

The Resolving Bereavement Book

The Caterpillar

- The Caterpillar in the story supports the children. The questions he asks and the way he listens are all done using counselling and mediation skills.

- Curly the Caterpillar does not judge people or take sides. His role is to use these skills to help the children resolve their own issues. This is done by listening to each person, asking questions and using these techniques to help the person think and learn about what they are feeling.

- Curly helps them to talk and express their feelings. This helps them find a way forward.

Stays Cool

Helps Find Solutions

Understands

Remains Impartial

Asks Good Questions

Doesn't Judge

Tool Box

The Resolving BEREAVEMENT Grief with your Child Book

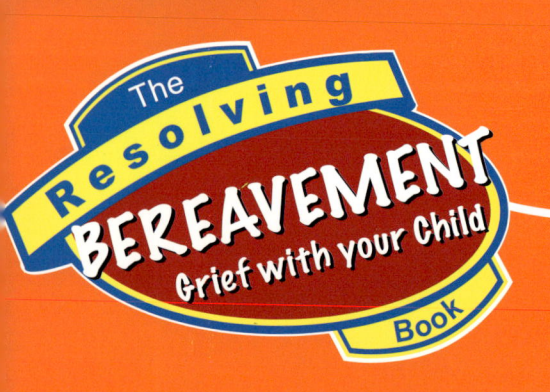

The Caterpillar Helps Because...

Listening helps calm kids.

Listening helps kids work things out for themselves.

Good questions help kids talk about what really bothers them.

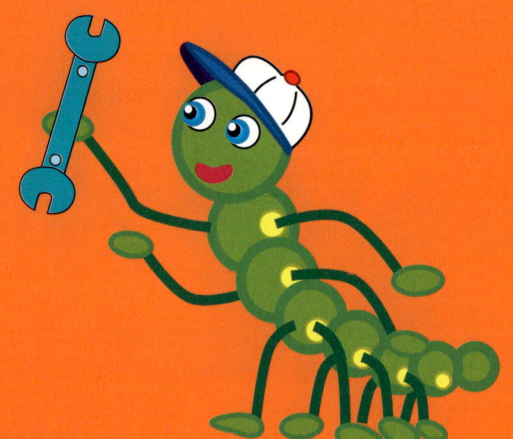

Focusing on them helps kids think about their own thoughts and feelings.

Helping kids sort things out for themselves helps them learn to adjust and move on.

The Resolving Bereavement Book

Skills used by the Caterpillar in this story:

1. **Listening** to how the children feel is an effective way of helping them. When the children felt listened to, they opened up and talked about what was really bothering them. It helped both of them to improve their ability to cope.

2. The **questions** the Caterpillar asks help them talk about what really bothers them and make a big difference in how they understand the real nature of their grief.

3. The Caterpillar does not talk about himself. **He concentrates on Lisa and Joe**. This means they have to focus on their own thoughts and feelings.

4. The Caterpillar helps the children **without making his own suggestions**. They learn more from doing it their way.

All the skills and ideas that the Caterpillar uses can be used by anyone reading this story to help them in their own lives.

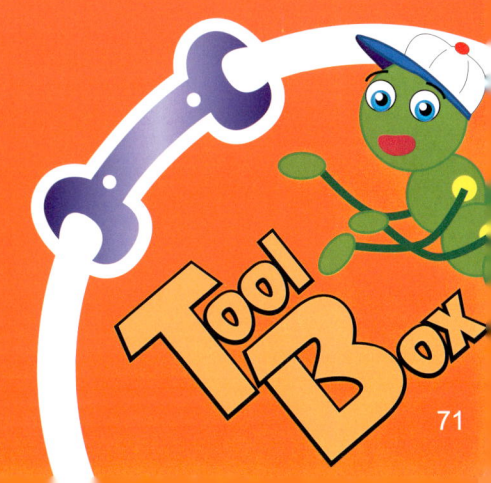

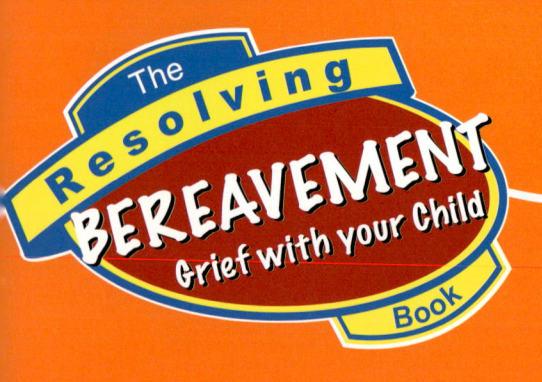

When We Lose Someone

- When we lose someone we feel very, very sad.

- We can feel ok and then we can have attacks of sadness.

- We can feel worried about the change that has happened.

- Grief can be like a sharp pain.

- Feelings of loss can change how we think about ourselves. We don't know how to act.

- We can stop liking ourselves.

- When we can't understand what has happened, we look for reasons to blame ourselves.

- We can feel very angry.

- Grief takes time to recover from. It is different for everybody.

- Slowly, we start to heal and feel better.

- We still miss the person we love but we know we will be alright.

www.resolvingbooks.com/whenwelosesomeone

The Resolving Bereavement Book

www.resolvingbooks.com/colourmein

Tool Box

73

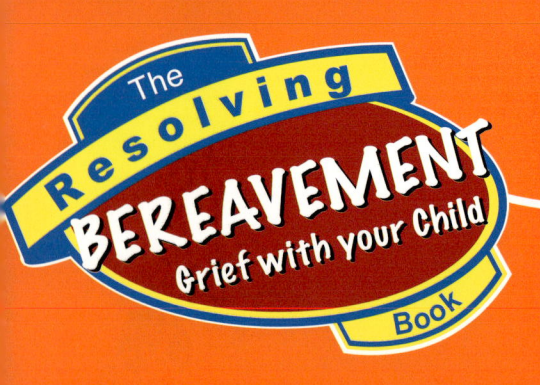

How People Feel on the Inside

When we are grieving our body can feel different. Sometimes our body can actually feel in pain. Our heart can feel as if it is breaking. This is our 'body alarm' telling us that we are not feeling good inside.

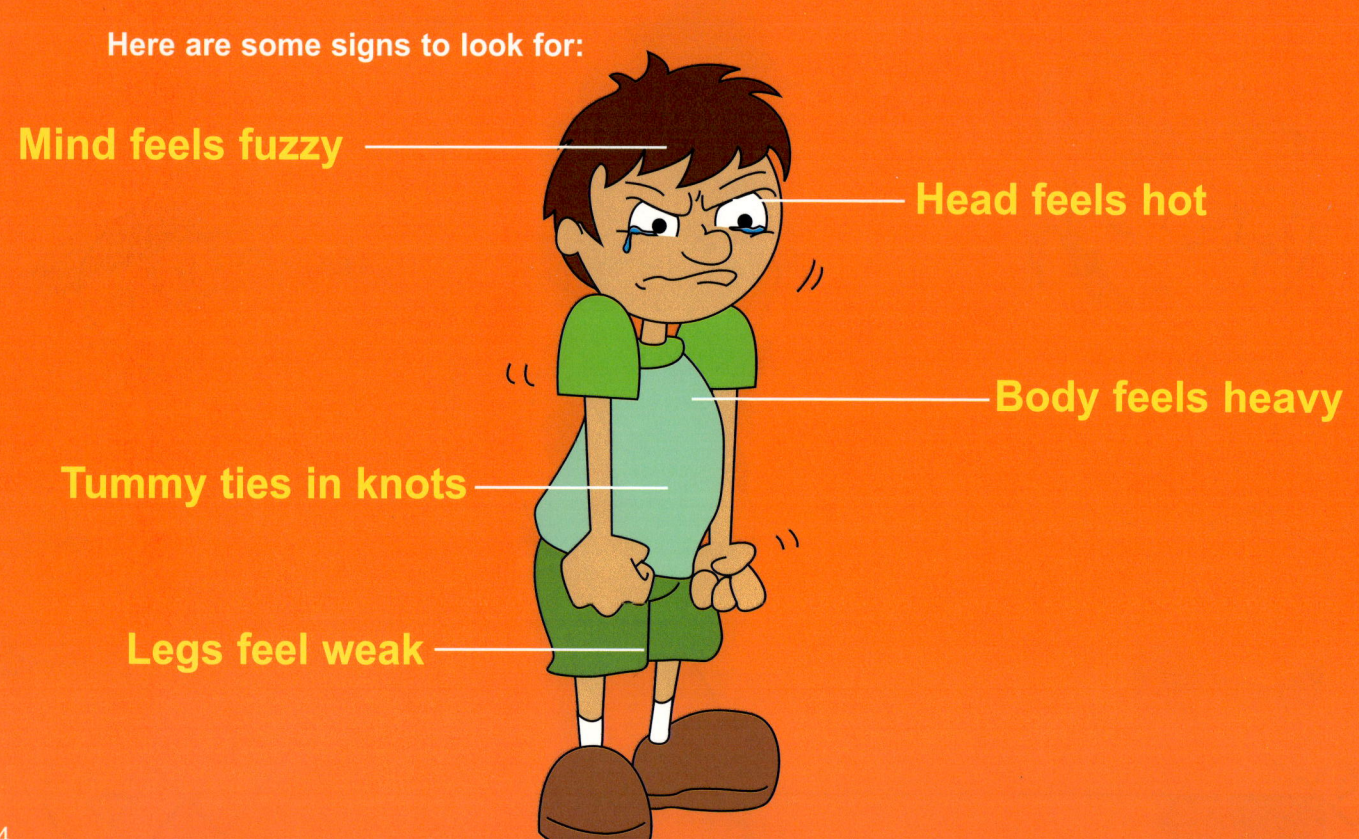

Here are some signs to look for:

Mind feels fuzzy

Head feels hot

Body feels heavy

Tummy ties in knots

Legs feel weak

The Resolving Bereavement Book

Which ones do you feel?

Remember, these are natural body reactions. Don't be frightened.

The next time you feel your body alarm going off:

1. Take slow, deep breaths.

2. Feel the adrenaline run through your body. Remember it will flow away again.

3. Take time out. Go for a walk, count down from ten...

4. Wait until you are calm before speaking.

More info VISIT
www.resolvingbooks.com/howpeoplefeelontheinside

Tool Box

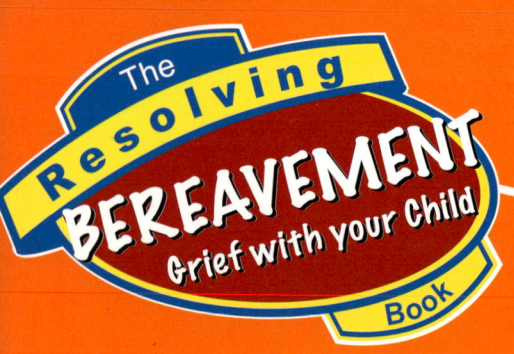

The Resolving BEREAVEMENT Grief with your Child Book

What People Do Not See

LISA

What we can see

What we can't see

The Resolving Bereavement Book

Remember that we don't always know how someone who is grieving is feeling or thinking. It is like looking at an iceberg and only seeing the tip.

We need to look below the water to find out the real story. We do that by listening and talking.

Here are some good questions to ask to help someone talk about how they really feel:

1. What happened?

2. What did you do?

3. What do you think about what happened?

4. How did you feel?

5. How are you now?

6. What do you think should happen next?

7. What do you want to do?

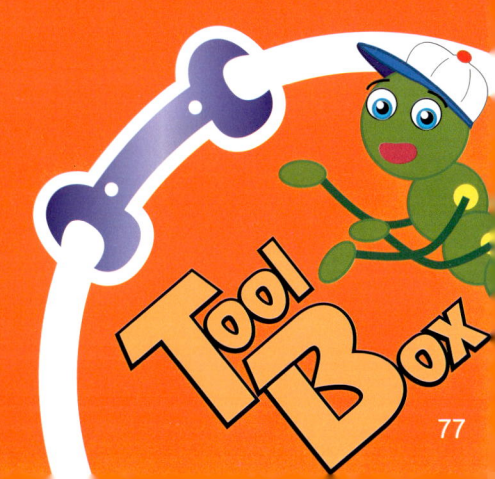

More info VISIT www.resolvingbooks.com/whatpeopledonotsee

Tool Box

Cooling Down

Inhale slowly

Exhale slowly

Now, what do I want to say?

The Resolving Bereavement Book

Anger

One of the feelings we can have when we lose someone we love is anger. It can be useful to have some skills to deal with this emotion:

- Breathing deeply and counting backwards from ten can help you cool down before deciding what to do.

- Counting backwards from ten, or even twenty, helps our brain calm down and start to think again.

- The adrenaline subsides and we can start talking more calmly about what has annoyed us.

Remember:

Our brain can stay in a heightened state for a number of hours after it has been triggered, even when we feel calmer. It is important to take a few minutes to cool down whenever you feel your anger building again.

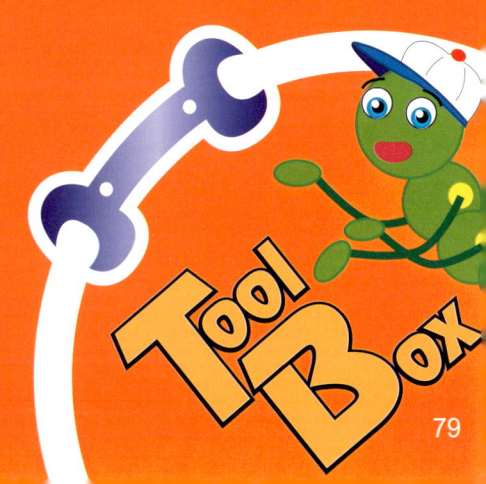

More info VISIT www.resolvingbooks.com/anger

More info VISIT www.resolvingbooks.com/measuringanger

Tool Box

Cool Down Checklist ✔

- [ ] Stop - take some long, deep breaths.
- [ ] Count slowly from ten to one.
- [ ] Breathe in through your nose and out through your mouth.
- [ ] Remember to think cool thoughts and not hot thoughts.
- [ ] Think of a happy place where you feel safe.
- [ ] Imagine a balloon filling with your anger and then deflating, releasing your anger.
- [ ] Find a pattern in the room (on the carpet, wallpaper) and trace around it with your eyes.
- [ ] Write down why you are angry.
- [ ] Go for a walk.
- [ ] Hug a large cushion.

When you have calmed down, you are ready to solve the problem.

The Resolving Bereavement Book

When we start to get angry and we can feel ourselves losing control, remember the Cool Down Checklist.

The more you use it, the more you will find it useful. It works because it helps our brain cool down and start to think again.

Why not...

Make your own checklist | **Download a template from www.resolvingbooks.com** | **Read this book**

...next time you feel angry.

Tool Box

The Resolving BEREAVEMENT Book
Grief with your Child

Listen and Talk

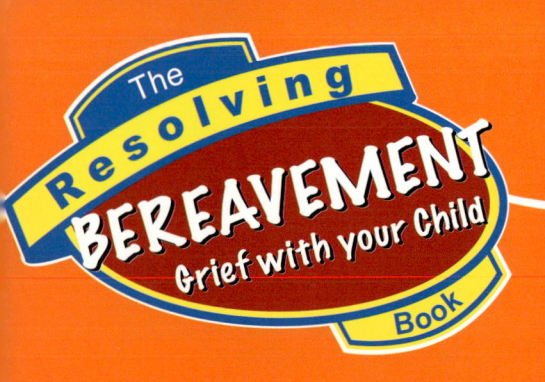

When someone is grieving we can find it hard to do the right thing.

We want to help, make things better, find a solution.

But sometimes all we can do is simply be there and listen.

Listening calms us down.

More info VISIT www.resolvingbooks.com/listenandtalk

The Resolving Bereavement Book

Listening finds better solutions.

We both win if we listen to each other.

Listening helps us feel better.

Tool Box

The Resolving BEREAVEMENT Grief with your Child Book

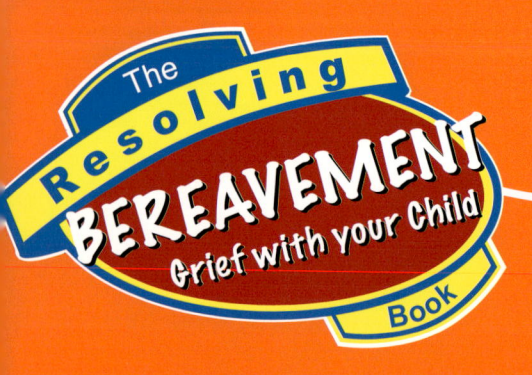

Listening and Talking

The most important thing to do when somebody is grieving is to listen to them.

As listeners, we need to help the other person express themselves better so that we can truly understand them.

What's wrong?	I don't know ▶	**You seem sad**	Yes, I'm unhappy
Tell me more	I had a bad day ▶	**What happened?**	I just miss Dad so much
Do you want to talk to me about it?	I feel so sad and lonely ▶	**Tell me more**	Well, I just wish he was here now
Is this the hardest thing?	Yes, it is. When I come home I feel saddest ▶	**What could we do now to help you feel better?**	I don't know. Maybe talking about him. Remembering the good times...

Remember:
It is important to talk about how you feel. Listening and talking helps us calm our minds and think more clearly. It can help us decide what to do.

The Resolving Bereavement Book

Powerful Questions

Asking questions can help us learn what is wrong. It can help the other person talk. Asking questions helps us resolve our arguments.

A powerful question is one that can help somebody think through a situation and figure out what to do.

There are many good questions. Here are some:

✓ **1. What has happened?**

✓ **2. What is wrong?**

✓ **3. What did you do?**

✓ **4. What did I do that upset you?**

✓ **5. Are you alright?**

✓ **6. What do you want to do now?**

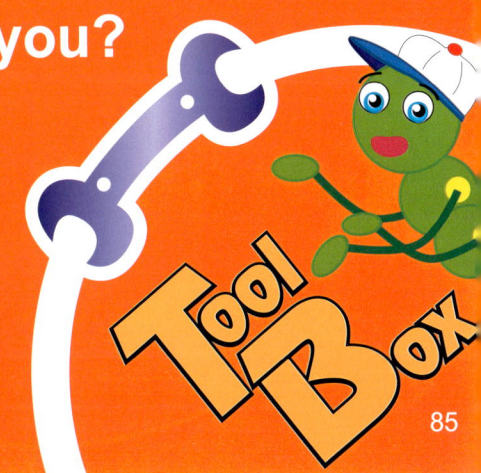

The Resolving BEREAVEMENT Book
Grief with your Child

Why Don't You Try These:

Have a special place to remember the people you love.

Keeping memories together helps us remember our lives.

More info VISIT www.resolvingbooks.com/whydontyoutrythese

The Resolving Bereavement Book

Painting pictures is a great way of expressing how you feel.

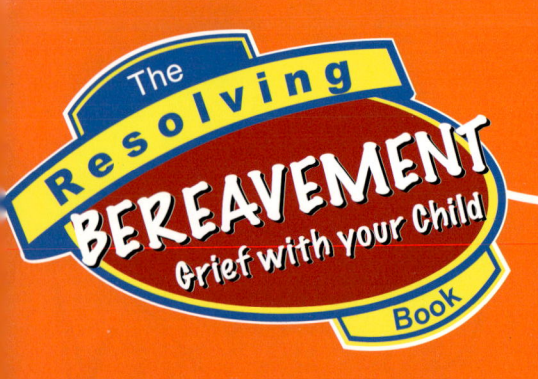

The Resolving BEREAVEMENT Grief with your Child Book

Learning to Feel Better Again

Grief is a natural reaction to loss. It can be difficult, but you will be alright.

Remember:

1. Feelings are a normal part of life. Don't be frightened of how you feel.

2. Talk to someone you trust about how you feel.

3. You *will* feel better in time.

More info VISIT www.resolvingbooks.com/learntofeelbetteragain